The FRENCH and INDIAN WAR

1660–1763

★★ *The Drama of* AMERICAN HISTORY ★★

The FRENCH *and* INDIAN WAR

1660–1763

Christopher Collier
James Lincoln Collier

BENCHMARK BOOKS

MARSHALL CAVENDISH
NEW YORK

ACKNOWLEDGMENT: The authors wish to thank Gregory Evans Dowd, Associate Professor of History, University of Notre Dame, for his careful reading of the text of this volume of The Drama of American History, and his thoughtful and useful comments. The work has been much improved by Professor Dowd's notes. The authors are deeply in his debt but, of course, assume full responsibility for the substance of the work, including any errors that may appear.

Photo research by James Lincoln Collier
COVER PHOTO: *Colonial Williamsburg Foundation*
PICTURE CREDITS: The photographs in this book are used by permission and through the courtesy of: *Corbis-Bettmann:* 10, 29, 46, 66, 71, 73, 74, 75. *Jamestown-Yorktown Educational Trust:* 11, 17, 77. *Colonial Williamsburg Foundation:* 18, 19, 20, 25, 26, 31, 37, 38 (top), 38 (bottom), 39, 40, 45, 48, 49, 50, 51, 52, 53, 55, 56 (left), 56 (right), 58 (all), 60, 63, 80.

AUTHORS' NOTE: The human beings who first peopled what we now call the Americas have traditionally been called *Indians,* because the first Europeans who landed in the Americas thought they had reached India. The term *Indians* is therefore not very accurate, and other terms have been used: *Amerinds,* and more recently, *Native Americans.* The Indians had no collective term for themselves. Today, most of them refer to themselves as Indians, and we will use that term here, while understanding that it is not very accurate.

Benchmark Books
Marshall Cavendish Corporation
99 White Plains Road
Tarrytown, New York 10591-9001

Library of Congress Cataloging-in-Publication Data

Collier, Christopher, date
The French and Indian War /
Christopher Collier, James Lincoln Collier.
p. cm. — (American History)
Includes bibliographical references and index.
ISBN 0-7614-0439-2 (lib. bdg.)
1. United States—History—French and Indian War, 1755–1763—Juvenile Literature. 2. United States—History—Colonial period, ca. 1600–1775—Juvenile literature.
I. Collier, James Lincoln, date. II. Title. III. Series.
E199.C7 1998   96-44063
973.2'6—dc21   CIP
                                                          AC
Printed in the United States of America

1 3 5 6 4 2

CONTENTS

Over many years of both teaching and writing for students at all levels, from grammar school to graduate school, it has been borne in on us that many, if not most, American history textbooks suffer from trying to include everything of any moment in the history of the nation. Students become lost in a swamp of factual information, and as a consequence lose track of how those facts fit together, and why they are significant and relevant to the world today.

In this series, our effort has been to strip the vast amount of available detail down to a central core. Our aim is to draw in bold strokes, providing enough information, but no more than is necessary, to bring out the basic themes of the American story, and what they mean to us now. We believe that it is surely more important for students to grasp the underlying concepts and ideas that emerge from the movement of history, than to memorize an array of facts and figures.

The difference between this series and many standard texts lies in what has been left out. We are convinced that students will better remember the important themes if they are not buried under a heap of names, dates, and places.

In this sense, our primary goal is what might be called citizenship education. We think it is critically important for America as a nation and Americans as individuals to understand the origins and workings of the public institutions which are central to American society. We have asked ourselves again and again what is most important for citizens of our democracy to know so they can most effectively make the system work for them and the nation. For this reason, we have focused on political and institutional history, leaving social and cultural history less well developed.

This series is divided into volumes that move chronologically through the American story. Each is built around a single topic, such as the pilgrims, the Constitutional Convention, or immigration. Each volume has been written so that it can stand alone, for students who wish to research a given topic. As a consequence, in many cases material from previous volumes is repeated, usually in abbreviated form, to set the topic in its historical context. That is to say, students of the Constitutional Convention must be given some idea of relations with England, and why the revolution was fought, even though the material was covered in detail in a previous volume. Readers should find that each volume tells an entire story that can be read with or without reference to other volumes.

Despite our belief that it is of the first importance to outline sharply basic concepts and generalizations, we have not neglected the great dramas of American history. The stories that will hold the attention of students are here, and we believe they will help the concepts they illustrate to stick in their minds. We think, for example, that knowing of Abraham Baldwin's brave and dramatic decision to vote with the small states at the Constitutional Convention will bring alive the Connecticut Compromise, out of which grew the American Senate.

Each of these volumes has been read by esteemed specialists in its particular topic; we have benefited from their comments.

CHAPTER I

The European Colonies in the Late Seventeenth Century

One of the most neglected periods in the modern history of North America is the period that began in the 1670s, when it was clear that the European colonies were in the country to stay, and ended in 1763 when, for reasons we shall see, the spirit of revolt against England began to stir. Everybody knows the stories and legends of the first settlers—the *Mayflower* and Plymouth Rock, John Smith and Pocahontas; and everybody remembers the great events of the 1770s and after—the Boston Tea Party, the Battles of Lexington and Concord, the signing of the Declaration of Independence.

But what happened in the hundred years between the time the land was settled and the start of the American Revolution is often forgotten. It should not be, for here the groundwork for the United States was laid. When the period began, the colonies in eastern North America consisted of scattered villages and towns up and down the seacoast, and perhaps up to fifty miles inland. Much of the land was still forest, inhabited by Indians living in their old ways. The human beings who first peopled what we now call the Americas have traditionally been called Indians, because the first Europeans who landed in the Americas thought they had

This picture is part of a famous series of engravings by a European named *Theodor de Bry, copied from watercolors painted in Virginia in 1585 by an Englishman, John White. Not all Indian villages in eastern America were surrounded by a palisade fence as shown here, but many were. Indians occupied most of the eastern area until well into the 1600s, long after the English began to settle there.*

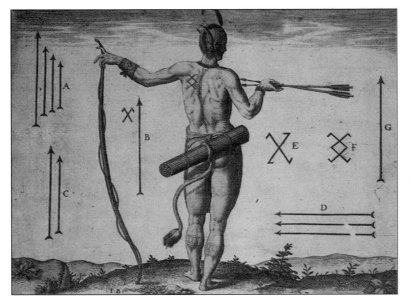

Another of the de Bry series, showing the decorative markings on the back of an Indian chief.

reached India. The term *Indians* is therefore not very accurate, and other terms have been used: *Amerinds*, and more recently, *Native Americans*. The Indians had no term for themselves, as they thought they were all the human beings that there were. Today most of them refer to themselves as Indians, and we will use that term here, while understanding that it is not very accurate. The colonies did not even have their own type of money, but used English shillings, Spanish dollars, French livres, and Dutch guldens. Mostly they did business without money at all, bartering so many pounds of tobacco for so much beef and butter. There were no newspapers and few books were published. There was little manufacturing. Paint, mirrors, clocks, windowpanes, hoes, needles, and most other manufactured goods had to be brought in from Europe, mainly from England.

Although, even in these early days, the colonists had a fair measure of influence over government—for the most part they set their own taxes—ultimate control rested in foreign governments. The English had the largest number of colonies, running from Hudson Bay at the top of the continent, down into the Caribbean islands. The French controlled much of what is now eastern Canada, and were developing outposts down the Mississippi and the territory around it. The Spanish held Florida, and claimed the immense tract of land from the Mississippi west to the Pacific, although they had colonized very little of it. The English had only recently taken over Manhattan Island and the Hudson River Valley from the Dutch, and the Dutch influence there remained great. There was, additionally, a little colony of Swedes in the area that is now Delaware. Control of the eastern seaboard of what would be the United States was still in dispute. There was, in fact, no certainty that it would develop into an English-speaking nation.

When the period ended in 1763, with the close of what we today call the French and Indian War, it had all changed drastically. Americans were now making a great many things for themselves, including axes, nails, sails, furniture. American-built ships were busily trading products like timber, livestock, food, furs, and tobacco to markets in the Caribbean, Europe, and Africa, and bringing back manufactured goods, molasses for rum, and, regrettably, slaves. Fortunes were being made in the import-export business, and wealthy people in cities like Boston, Philadelphia, and Charleston were building grand houses and furnishing them with gilt mirrors, carved chests, silk drapes from Europe.

Along the seacoast much of the forest had been cut off and turned into villages and farms, and the Indians had been driven out. Settlers were pushing into the "backcountry" and then climbing over the Appalachian Mountains into the land beyond, once again contesting the Indians for possession of the forests and fields. Colonial printers were publishing books, newspapers, almanacs. There was an adequate mail service, at least between the seacoast cities.

The area was no longer in dispute. In 1763, the whole of North America, from Hudson Bay to Florida, from the Atlantic to the Missis-

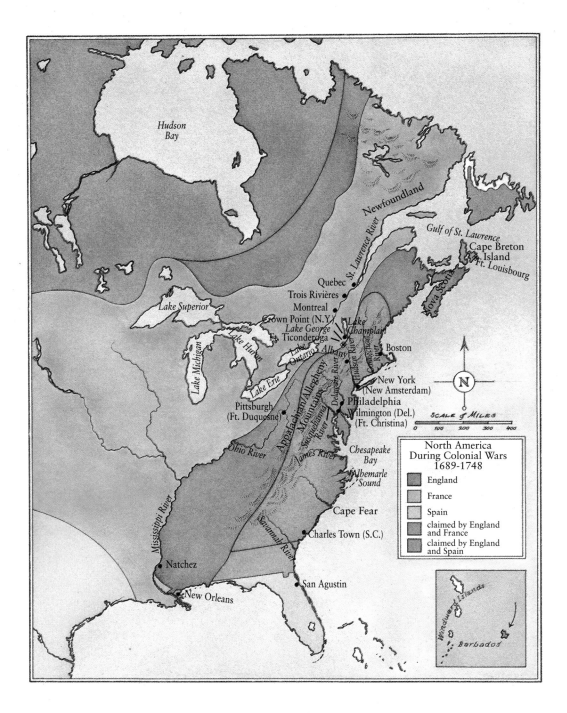

North America
During Colonial Wars
1689-1748

England
France
Spain
claimed by England
and France
claimed by England
and Spain

Hudson
Bay

Newfoundland

St. Lawrence River

Gulf of St. Lawrence

Cape Breton
Island
Ft. Louisbourg

Quebec
Trois Rivières
Montreal

Lake Superior

Crown Point (N.Y.)
Lake George
Ft. Ticonderoga

Lake
Champlain

Nova Scotia

Lake Michigan

Lake Huron

Lake
Ontario

Albany

Hudson River

Connecticut River

Boston

Lake Erie

New York
(New Amsterdam)

Pittsburgh
(Ft. Duquesne)

Appalachian
Mountains

Allegheny

Delaware River

Philadelphia
Wilmington (Del.)
(Ft. Christina)

N

SCALE of MILES
0   100   200   300   400

Ohio River

Susquehanna
River

James River

Chesapeake
Bay

Albemarle
Sound

Mississippi River

Cape Fear

Savannah River

Charles Town (S.C.)

Natchez

New Orleans

San Agustin

Windward Islands

Barbados

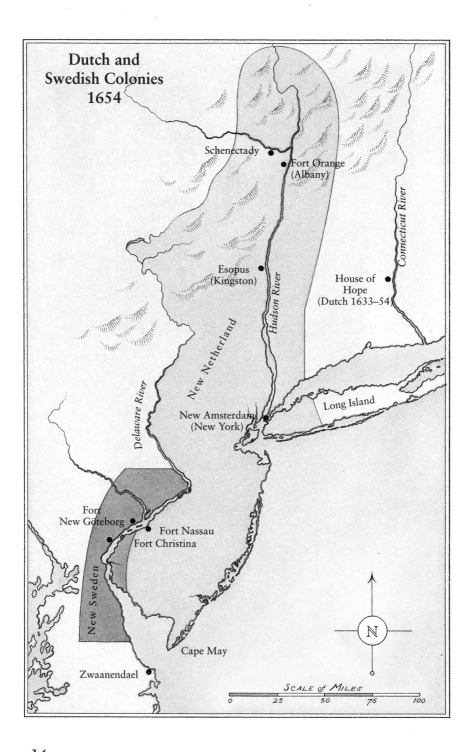

Dutch and
Swedish Colonies
1654

Schenectady
Fort Orange
(Albany)

Esopus
(Kingston)

House of
Hope
(Dutch 1633–54)

Connecticut River

Hudson River

New Netherland

Delaware River

New Amsterdam
(New York)

Long Island

Fort
New Göteborg
Fort Nassau
Fort Christina

New Sweden

Cape May

Zwaanendael

N

SCALE of MILES

0   25   50   75   100

sippi, was controlled by one nation—Great Britain. Although some Americans still spoke Dutch, French, Spanish, Swedish, or German, the bulk of the population spoke English. The colonies operated by laws and customs mainly derived from English ones and the people frequently followed English fashions in dress, cooking, and home decoration. But—and this is the critical *but*—many of them had begun to see themselves as special Englishmen, American Englishmen, different from Englishmen in England. And why should they not? Some of the young people growing up along the seacoast had grandfathers whose own grandfathers had lived only in America.

Clearly, a great deal happened in America during the hundred-year period we are looking at. We can see two great themes. The first was what historians call the "maturing" of America, as the collection of colonies went from rough frontier settlements to well-established, organized communities of villages, towns, and even cities, trading among themselves as well as with foreign lands. The second theme was the conflict between various European powers for control of North America and its vast potential wealth.

We are going to look at these two developments side by side. They happened gradually, step by step. A change that takes place a bit at a time is sometimes hard to get a grip on. It will help to understand that Europeans, at the outset, had no elaborate plans for the development of North America. They were just going along trying to take advantage of whatever possibilities they saw, without any long-range schemes in mind. It has been said that the British Empire was founded in a "fit of absent-mindedness."

In fact, the idea is true of most of the European colonies. For a long time after Columbus first touched down in the New World, the Europeans saw America only as a place to be stripped of its raw materials—gold and silver in Spanish America, furs in the northern parts of North America, fish from the Atlantic. Only slowly did they begin to settle the New World with Europeans (and African slaves), and that, once again, was for the purpose of bringing valuable goods back to London, Paris, Amsterdam—sugar from the Caribbean islands, tobacco from Virginia, rice from the Carolinas, timber from everywhere. The European rulers and their court of officials had no idea that they were laying the foundations for half a world of new nations. As a consequence, they did not give much thought as to how these strange faraway places should be settled, how they should be governed, who should live there—just so long as the fur, tobacco, and fish kept flowing in.

However haphazardly it was done, by the 1660s or 1670s, Europeans had established several colonies on the Atlantic Coast that looked as if they were going to survive. The two most important of them were the colonies in Massachusetts and Virginia, the first to be founded on the North American seaboard. The Massachusetts Bay colony had overflowed into Connecticut, up into what are now Maine and New Hampshire, and eventually farther south onto Long Island. A number of religious dissenters, many of them with extreme views, were forced to leave Massachusetts and gravitated to Narragansett Bay, where they started settling what is now Rhode Island. These New England colonies continued to have trouble with the Indians whom they were displacing, especially on the western frontier, around the Connecticut River, but by the 1670s they were solidly established, and growing prosperous. (For the story of the settlement of New England readers can consult *Pilgrims and Puritans,* the third book of this series.)

The older Virginia colony was growing even more prosperous on tobacco. The colonists here were pushing westward, and generally around the Chesapeake Bay area down into what would be North Carolina, and up into the future Maryland. (The story of Virginia's founding is told in *The Paradox of Jamestown,* the second book of this series.)

Sweden, too, was trying to share in the wealth coming out of the New *(right) Jamestown in the early 1600s was a rough place. Houses were thatched, streets were unpaved, and cooking was done over wood fires. The job of chopping wood was never ending.*

(bottom) Even in the late 1600s, the threat of an Indian attack remained, and farm workers usually had an armed guard with them. In this re-creation, settlers are working a tobacco field outside Jamestown.

By the early 1700s, North America was an entirely different place. The Bruton Parish church, built in 1715 in Williamsburg, is one of the oldest existing church buildings in the United States. Williamsburg, then the capital of Virginia, has been carefully restored. The small white building in the foreground was probably a kitchen. Wealthy people usually had their kitchen in a separate building to avoid the smells of cooking and the heat from the big fireplace.

World, and had established a small colony in what is now Wilmington, Delaware, which they called Fort Christina. This colony, too, however small, was thriving.

Yet another colony, called Maryland, had been founded in the northern part of the Chesapeake Bay area. It had been established as a haven for Roman Catholics, who were under pressure in England to join the official Church of England. It was a "proprietary" colony, meaning that it was owned lock, stock, and barrel by one individual, who could run it more or less as he pleased. The original proprietor, Lord Baltimore, never

The Virginia governor's palace in Williamsburg was an extremely elegant building, attesting to the wealth and stability of the colony, which was growing rich on tobacco and other crops. It was built in 1722 and is shown here in the snow.

visited his own province, and as a consequence it grew up more haphazardly than did some of the other colonies. Lord Baltimore was succeeded by his son, Charles Calvert, who lived in the colony and was its governor,

By the later 1700s, Americans had time for art and entertainment. This 1771 painting, by the famous artist Charles Willson Peale, shows an actress playing the part of Fidele in Shakespeare's Cymbeline.

and he tried to rule with a strong hand. Calvert and other officials of Maryland were Roman Catholics, while many of the colonists—eventually a majority of them—were Protestants. Inevitably, there was friction. But the colony, like Virginia, was growing prosperous on tobacco.

Between the Chesapeake Bay settlements and the New England colonies there lay millions of acres of rich land filled with game, bordered by the Atlantic Ocean filled with fish. It was also watered by a number of rivers, including the ones we now call the Hudson and the Delaware. Rivers were critically important to the settling of America. Most of the land was forested, despite many Indian cornfields. Traveling through the country was troublesome and could be dangerous if you met hostile Indians or wild animals like wolves, who most believed would as soon eat humans as deer. Carrying sacks of corn or bundles of fur through the forests was next to impossible. In North America, people and goods moved by water on ships and small boats up and down the coast from port to port and on rivers inland. Rivers like the James, the Connecticut, the St. Lawrence were essential roads into the interior, by which settlers could move inland to carve out farms, and fur traders could carry out beaver pelts and deerskins. The existence of two great rivers and many lesser ones in the relatively unsettled area between New England and Chesapeake Bay made the region especially attractive.

The English had laid claim to the area, but claims by European powers to huge tracts of land meant nothing unless they could gain control of them. The Dutch also claimed the area. Holland, in the 1700s, was a major force in international trade. It had excellent ships and skilled sailors, and had created a trading network in what was called the East Indies—that is, the area we now call Southeast Asia. The spices and other goods they were bringing out of the East were far more valuable than the tobacco and codfish shipped from North America, and Holland was slow to get started there.

But in 1609, the Dutch signed up an English sea captain named Henry

Hudson to do some exploring for them. Hudson had already discovered the river named for him, and the Dutch hoped it would prove to be the much sought water route through the American continent to the East Indies. Hudson went up the river until he could go no farther, and staked out a claim for his employers to all the lands adjoining the Hudson River.

For a long time the Dutch, preoccupied by the wealth pouring in from the East Indies, ignored their North American claim. But as it became clear that the French and English were profiting from their colonies, the Dutch began to take Hudson's claim more seriously. In 1624, they started a small colony at what is now Albany, which they called Fort Orange, mainly to trade with the Indians for furs. The next year a group of Dutchmen landed on an island at the mouth of the Hudson, which they purchased from the Manhates Indians, who in fact did not own it themselves.

The Dutch saw that they would not be able to hang on to the territory unless it was peopled, and they set up a system giving a huge piece of land to anyone who could settle fifty families on it. Only a few of these "patroons" actually managed to set up their patroonships; nonetheless, the Dutch colony began to fill up, not only on the Hudson River lands claimed by Henry Hudson, but in other places where the English thought they held sway, such as Long Island, and along the Delaware. The Dutch also built some trading posts on the Connecticut River at modern day Hartford and Saybrook.

To sum up, the situation in eastern North America in the years around 1660–1670 was this: the Spanish claimed most of the land west of the Mississippi, but had done little with it; aside from their small military posts in Florida the French held the St. Lawrence Seaway area, were building posts down the Mississippi, and were claiming much of the land between the Mississippi and the Appalachian Mountains; the Dutch—who in 1655 took Fort Christina from the Swedes—held the Hudson River Valley until 1664, and had claims elsewhere; the English had a considerable number of settlements in New England, on Long Island, and around Chesapeake Bay. Five nations were crowding themselves onto the Atlantic seaboard, jostling each other for room. A showdown was inevitable. That contest for North America is the essential story of this part of American history.

CHAPTER II

The Dutch and the English in America

To understand this confused and confusing period in American history, we should step away a little and view the situation as it was seen from Europe. In fact, a lot of the confusion that existed in America was due to the fact that Europe itself was in a state of considerable confusion. The nations we know today as Italy and Germany did not exist as such, but were collections of quarreling princedoms and duchies that happened to use the same languages. The more powerful nations, especially England, Spain, France, and Holland, were if anything more quarrelsome, again and again fighting wars among themselves, forming alliances, and then fighting once again. To these states the game was being played in Europe, not America, and the game was, simply put, King of the Hill. The whole idea was to get the upper hand, if possible; but at the least, not to let anyone else have the upper hand. The colonies were seen only as useful tools in the fight. Mainly, that meant wrestling wealth out of them in order to pay the fearful expenses of the wars that playing King of the Hill led European nations into.

These European nations saw the colonies as "theirs," to do with as they liked. How the colonists felt about it did not interest them very

The status of the Indians changed rapidly as America matured in the late seventeenth and early eighteenth centuries. Many natives were driven out, many were killed in wars, and many died of European diseases. Most tribes entered into arrangements with European powers, particularly the English and French. In 1762 these Cherokee Indians visited London to pay homage to "The King, Our Father." Note their European finery, which they would have obtained in trade for furs.

much. In fact, their lack of interest was general. Even quite sophisticated European diplomats, who could find their ways around the great cities of Europe with ease, had only the haziest idea of American geography. They often carved up huge chunks of land along lines that had little to do with the rivers, mountains, and lakes that lay there. Early grants, as in the case of Massachusetts, were made "from sea to sea" by monarchs who hadn't the foggiest idea of how far it was from the Atlantic to the Pacific. The same pieces of land were often given to different parties: for example, the Wyoming Valley area of Pennsylvania was given by Charles II to both Connecticut and Pennsylvania.

If the needs and desires of the colonists did not concern European rulers very much, the interests of the people the Europeans hoped to shove aside—the Indians—mattered to them even less. There were millions of Indians in North America living in a rich variety of cultures that had been growing for at least twelve thousand years—the wealthy people of the Northwest who carved the famous twenty-foot-tall totem poles, and in great boats hunted the seas for large animals; the Indians of the plains who hunted buffalo and made war on each other almost as a sport; the northeastern Indians such as the Algonquian and Iroquois who farmed, hunted, and fished, and

It is not well understood that many Indians did not leave their old lands, but stayed and adapted to European ways. Denny Soccabesan was one who stayed. This portrait is thought by historians to be accurate, and it shows how much she had adapted to European ways.

also played King of the Hill among themselves as much as the Europeans did.

The Indians were seen by policy makers in Europe as at best a nuisance, and at worst potential slaves who could be forced to work to make the Europeans richer. Most Europeans felt that the Indians ought to be turned into Christians, and some of them sent missionaries over to convert them. Others assumed that the Indians would see the benefits of European civilization, and would quickly adopt European ways, learning to farm and build little villages like the ones in Europe. Still others believed that the Indians should simply be driven away. Whatever the view, few Europeans had any compunction about doing what they liked with the Indians. (As it turned out, the Indians were able to keep the Europeans out of North America for more than a century after the voyages of Columbus. For that story, see *Clash of Cultures,* the first book of this series.)

In defense of the Europeans, it must be pointed out that neither the Indians nor people elsewhere in the world that the Europeans wanted to exploit—like Africans or Indonesians—were any more charitable to their neighbors. Conquest is a universal fact in human life, and Africans and Asians were just as guilty of slaughtering or enslaving their defeated enemies as the Europeans were. Nonetheless, it took the Europeans a long while to develop a realistic understanding of the Indians and how to deal with them.

The colonies, then, were seen as a sideshow to the main events taking place in Europe. The rulers of Europe saw the widespread and disparate colonies as pawns in the great game of nation building. Indeed, by 1660 or so, they were only beginning to grasp the idea that they were creating colonial empires. They were simply looking to take what wealth they could from the newly discovered lands, mainly in order to play King of the Hill at home. The colonies, really, were only pieces in the larger game.

That was certainly true of the Dutch. The land they claimed in the

Hudson Valley was some of the finest country on the Atlantic Coast of North America. The soil was fertile, the great river system centered on the Hudson offered a broad roadway into the interior, and at its mouth was one of the finest harbors anywhere in the world. Yet the Dutch were extremely slow to do anything with it. They called their colony New Netherland. Its governor was the tough Peter Minuit, who ruled with an iron hand. He built a fort and a tiny village on the southern tip of Manhattan, which he called New Amsterdam. Other Dutch trading posts were pulled together on the Hudson at Fort Orange, now Albany, up the Connecticut River, and on the Delaware. Nonetheless, despite an offer to give as much as one hundred thousand acres to patroons, the region remained mostly empty. (An acre is slightly smaller than a football field.) The Dutch colonists occupied Manhattan and places around it, and a few spots along the Hudson. Most of Long Island, which the Dutch claimed, was filling up with English from Connecticut.

The little colony struggled along until 1647, when the now legendary Peter Stuyvesant was brought in as governor. A one-legged, tough, blunt-spoken man, he liked to run things his own way. He was faced with many problems, some of them unsolvable. Among other things, he was badly outnumbered by the English in nearby Long Island and Connecticut. In his capital city, New Amsterdam, there were four hundred denizens who spoke eighteen different languages.

But despite everything, Stuyvesant managed to make the little colony work. He built up a lucrative fur trade with the Indians through his outposts up the Hudson. He made New Amsterdam a major seaport, through which flowed American products from many colonies, including tobacco, fish, and timber, which was shipped to Holland for resale. He developed facilities for repairing and outfitting Dutch merchant ships for further trips.

New Amsterdam was a great annoyance to the English. They had come to think of North America—its eastern seaboard, at least—as

An undated woodcut of Peter Stuyvesant of New York, negotiating with some Indians. The picture is an artist's later version of the event.

theirs. They had already settled good-sized chunks of it, and were in the process of settling more. The English wanted no Dutch colony set down in the middle of their America.

Now European rivalries spilled over into the New World. The English were threatened by the great successes of the Dutch in the East Indies because riches could be turned into military strength. The Dutch were also doing a lot of business in America, buying tobacco, fish, and other products from the English colonists, who were more concerned with getting the best price for their goods than patriotically selling only to English merchants. In 1651, the government in London passed the first of what came to be known as the Navigation Acts, to stop trade between Holland and the English colonists. Tension between the two nations was building up, and in 1652, war broke out between them, the first of what would be three Anglo-Dutch wars over the next twenty-two years.

These wars were generally inconclusive, but they kept the English and the Dutch in America perpetually quarreling with each other. Stuyvesant was always arguing with the English people living in Manhattan or on the areas of Long Island he claimed for the Dutch. He also had the Swedes to worry about, for they were cutting deeply into the fur trade. In 1655, he led a small force against them, and put them under Dutch rule.

Back in London a new version of the exploration of the Hudson River area was being peddled around: Henry Hudson, after all, had been English. Some Indians said they had seen the English flag flying over Manhattan. Hudson, so the story went, had then illegally sold Manhattan to the Dutch. Conveniently forgotten was the fact that the Dutch, not the English, had hired Hudson to make the trip in the first place. The public began to get steamed up; and so did English businessmen when they were told that the Dutch were shipping "above 100,000 beaver skins" out of New Amsterdam each year.

The English king at this point was Charles II, a lazy and pleasure-loving man who liked going to the theater and visiting his girlfriends

Under English rule, by 1763 New York had become a very prosperous port, with many fine buildings. Here it is shown from what is now Brooklyn Heights.

more than governing. Charles's younger brother James, the duke of York, was a much more serious man, with a religious bent. James was trying to bring some order out of his brother's American colonies. Charles was not very compatible with James, but he realized that in all fairness he ought to do something for him. He asserted the English claim to the Hudson Valley area, and gave it all to James, and threw in with it an area that included pieces of Maine, Connecticut, Delaware, and all of New Jersey.

In 1664, James, Duke of York, now set about claiming his property. He put together a small fleet and an army of three hundred men under the command of an extremely competent soldier, Richard Nicolls, and sent them off to take New Netherland away from the Dutch.

In America, the irascible one-legged Stuyvesant picked up rumors that the English fleet was on its way. Hastily he began to improvise his defenses. There was not enough of anything in the city to withstand a siege— not enough flour, not enough beer, not enough gunpowder, and certainly not enough fighting men. But Stuyvesant was no coward, and when Nicolls's fleet showed up in the harbor he was prepared to fight.

But the people of New Amsterdam were not. A bloody battle, in which they and their families might be slaughtered, their houses burned, their little fortunes stolen, was the last thing they wanted. Further, rumors had it that settlers from Long Island were gathering in Brooklyn, across the river, in order to plunder the town when Nicolls moved in.

Stuyvesant's position was desperate, and Nicolls knew it. He sent a message to Stuyvesant ordering him to surrender. Stuyvesant refused. Next Nicolls sent over emissaries with a letter stating terms. When Stuyvesant read the letter he instantly realized that Nicolls's terms were very generous, saying in effect that the Dutch citizens could go on pretty much as they always had, except they would live under an English flag, and trade with Holland would be controlled. Stuyvesant knew perfectly well that if the townspeople knew of these generous terms they would insist on surrendering. He tore the letter up.

Then he stumped off on his wooden leg to the fort, and climbed up onto the gun platform. A gunner stood there with a light, ready to fire a cannon shot at the English ships. A crowd below stared up in fear. Then two old friends of Stuyvesant came out of the crowd, and climbed up onto the platform. "Taking him gently by the arms [they] led him away."

It was over, and Stuyvesant knew it. He went back to his office. One of his assistants managed to piece the torn letter together, and soon terms were agreed to. New Netherland would now be New York. The Dutch trading post up the Hudson would be Albany, after another title James held. And Stuyvesant? For him, Manhattan was home, and he retired to his farm there, devoting his time and attention to his land and his family. There was a postscript: some ten years later the Dutch recaptured the city of New York almost by accident; but they were not prepared to hold it, and shortly thereafter it reverted to the English for good.

The Dutch, nonetheless, were the majority there, and continued to set the tone, especially for Albany up the Hudson and for what was now called New York City—the little town at the foot of Manhattan Island. Dutch was the main language, and a lot of their customs remained. It was the Dutch who brought the Easter egg, ice-skating, and St. Nicholas to America, and they gave us many words like "Yankees," "cookie," "yacht," "boss," and "stoop." Nonetheless, with the bloodless victory, Nicolls, his handful of ships, and three hundred men, had eliminated one of the European rivals for power in North America. This episode shows how offhand the Europeans were about the American colonies. With a few hundred men and two or three ships the Dutch could have hung on to what would eventually be an immensely profitable colony. But they did not bother.

The players in the North American game had now been reduced by two, the Dutch and the Swedes. The remaining contestants were the Spanish, English, and French.

CHAPTER III

The Spanish Retreat

The Dutch conquest of the Swedes and the English conquest of the Dutch reduced the European contestants for control of North America to three: England, France, and Spain.

The Spanish settlement at St. Augustine was small and mainly a fort. It nonetheless provided a base from which the Spanish could, and from time to time did, attach English and French settlements on the Atlantic and Gulf coasts. Huge areas north and west lay open to Spanish expansion, and Franciscan missionaries won many friends and potential allies among the Indians there.

The area to the north of Spanish Florida along the Atlantic Coast had always attracted the attention of English investors. Its winters were much milder than those of New England, and as a consequence it had a longer growing season. The soil was good—indeed, stories got back to England that the land produced enough food for settlers to live on without cultivation. But there were drawbacks: settlements were open to attack by the Spanish to the south, and there was no good natural harbor in the northern part of the territory, below the Virginia borderline. And there was always the Indian threat.

During the years after 1660, several wealthy Englishmen made plans to settle the area, now called Carolina, for Charles II. A small colony around Cape Fear just south of Virginia was set up by some migrating New Englanders, but it quickly collapsed.

Then a group of major lords, who had substantial influence with Charles, combined to settle the area. They believed that subtropical products like wine, olives, and silk could be produced there, and stipulated that such goods would go untaxed for seven years, for those who would try the experiment. The investors believed that they need not send out colonists from England: there were plenty of people in the New World, particularly in Barbados, who were looking for fresh land to develop. They managed to set up a colony of Barbadians in the Cape Fear region in 1664. But through bad luck this colony also failed.

Now Sir Anthony Ashley Cooper, soon to become earl of Shaftesbury, stepped forward. He persuaded the proprietors to put in more money, and with the aid of the famous philosopher John Locke, drew up a complex and impractical constitution for the colony. Shaftesbury's efforts worked. A settlement was established at Albemarle Point. A small Spanish fleet came up the coast to drive the settlers out, but a lucky storm swept the ships away. In 1680, a group of French Protestants called Huguenots, who were being persecuted at home, arrived, and the next year a small group of Scots came. Once again the Spanish attacked and burned the little village the Scots had established, but they persisted, and rebuilt the village.

A second settlement was also established in the south, close to Spanish Florida, at the junction of the Ashley and Cooper Rivers, both named for Shaftesbury. This town was known as Charles Town (now Charleston), and it, too, survived. By 1700, there were three thousand settlers in the Albemarle region to the north, and five thousand spreading out from Charles Town in the south.

The Appalachian mountain chain acted as an even more formidable barrier to western expansion than in the more northern colonies, but nevertheless as the population of the colony grew, settlers pushed westward, into territory the French and Spanish had thought of as their own. Here the Carolina settlers made contact with the Indians and entered the very profitable trade in fur and deer hides, which in time would bring them into competition with French traders coming down the Mississippi from their base on the St. Lawrence. The French had made great efforts to stay on good terms with the Indians, while the English had often gone to war with them. Nonetheless, the English were willing to pay more in trade goods than the French were, and a lot of fur and deer hides began to flow through the booming port of Charles Town. The inland settlers also traded in Indian slaves, most of whom were sent to Barbados. More important, the settlers in the Charles Town area learned to cultivate rice as well as indigo, which was used for making blue dyes. The Carolina planters found a ready market for their goods, particularly food, in the Caribbean, especially Barbados. Here people were growing rich on sugar. They were using every available scrap of land for sugarcane, and consequently had to import much of their food. From Carolina the trip to Barbados was relatively short. They would sell their rice, pork, corn, and cattle, then load up with sugar and ginger, which they would carry to England. Here they would pick up the manufactured goods—furniture, glassware, nails, and tools—that were so desperately needed in the new colonies, and carry them home. This trade was very lucrative, and soon Charles Town became one of the most prosperous ports on the North Atlantic coast. By the early 1700s, the English were solidly established in Carolina.

Carolina remained a single colony for some years. But there was increasing friction between religious and political groups in the colony. Wars with the Indians and other troubles caused the English king to detach Albemarle and establish it as a separate colony of North Carolina in 1712.

There remained a strip of land between South Carolina and Spanish

South Carolina quickly grew into a wealthy and powerful colony. This is the earliest known picture of Charles Town (Charleston), then growing rich on exports of rice and indigo grown with slave labor. The picture was painted in the 1730s.

Florida. In 1733, James Oglethorpe, acting for some British philanthropists, sent a group of settlers into this piece of land, near the mouth of the Savannah River. The British founders of the colony hoped to fill it with people who had been imprisoned for debt in England. (At that time you could be jailed for running up debts until your friends and family could pay off what you owed.) The assumption was that debtors set up on farms in America would earn enough to pay their creditors.

As in the Carolinas, the trustees of the new colony, which they called Georgia, after George II, thought that wine, olives, and silk could be produced there. Products of this kind did not need slave labor. The trustees were fearful that the early Spanish might aid slaves to revolt against their English masters, and they banned slavery from Georgia. The trustees also banned the importation of rum and brandy.

Neither of these regulations sat well with the colonists. As had so fre-

(left) Growing American prosperity was dependent on an enormous amount of hard work. In this re-creation a worker packs tobacco, the main source of Virginia's wealth, into a barrel.

(bottom) It took great skill for cabinetmakers, using only hand tools like these, to turn out fine furniture, doors, and windows.

quently been the case in America, what the investors hoped the settlers would do was different from what the settlers wanted for themselves. In this case the colonists—many of whom had migrated down from South Carolina—wanted to grow wealthy in the same way as the other southern colonies had, by using slave labor to grow cash crops for export. The ban on rum particularly rankled them. Rum was useful in trading for slaves, and was made from sugarcane produced in Barbados. The ban on rum interfered with a potentially profitable trade with Barbados.

As in Carolina, the Georgia backcountry was open to expansion, and the settlers began to move west, where they traded with the Indians for furs, and scratched farms out of the wilderness.

Much of the labor, especially in the south, was provided by slaves. In this reenactment, two slaves cut some of the endless supply of wood Americans needed for their fires.

A re-creation of slaves' quarters with a fenced-in yard, where they might grow vegetables or even keep a chicken or pig in such spare time as they had.

The development of these English southern colonies had a substantial effect on the other two contestants for North America. With their growing population leaking into the backcountry, Carolina and Georgia blocked Spanish expansion out of Florida and the Gulf coast up to the north. If the Spanish had wanted to make a real fight of it, they might have driven the English out of the lands to the north of Florida. Spain had declined in strength and influence since its days of glory a century earlier, when it had been the mightiest power in Europe; nonetheless, it was still a wealthy nation and had the money and men to make a fight of it in North America.

But basically, the Spanish were not interested, though they summoned the will and resources to fend off repeated English attacks against San Marcos in northern Florida. They had enormous holdings west of the Mississippi and in Mexico, the Caribbean, Central and South America. Their meager settlements in North America seemed insignificant. Why bother with them? For the history of the United States, the elimination of Spain as a contestant for power in North America was critically important. Had Spain managed to make a real fight of it, Latin America might now begin at the southern border of Virginia, with who knows what consequences for the history of the lands to the north.

For the French, too, these new colonies were troublesome. The English settlers there were making heavy inroads in the fur trade with the Indians, which the French had previously had to themselves. The French efforts to keep the English out of the fur trade would have considerable consequences in due time.

CHAPTER IV

Pennsylvania on the Delaware River

We have been looking at one of the two great movements that took place in the Americas during the hundred or so years between the time when the first colonies were firmly established, and the end of the French and Indian War in 1763—that is, the struggle between several European powers for control of the North American continent. Now we must turn to the second theme—the maturing of the colonies as they turned from outposts of Europe into a land with a society and culture of its own. In order to make sense of this confused and confusing time, we shall look at the progress of one colony, Pennsylvania, while bearing in mind that all the colonies were special in certain ways.

We will begin with an Englishman named William Penn. He was very well connected. His father had been an admiral in the British navy, and helpful to both Charles II and his brother James, the duke of York, who was himself to be king one day. Admiral Penn expected great things of his son William. But William, like many other people, got caught up in the religious fervor heating up around him. He joined the most radical of the Protestant sects, the Quakers. They believed that all people were equal in the eyes of God, an idea that did not suit those in power. They were pacifists, which nearly was treason in a nation that was regularly at war. They refused to take oaths. They believed in "plainness" in speech and dress, at a time when the rich and powerful dressed like peacocks in silks and jewels. They called their church a "meetinghouse," in which anyone could speak. Most particularly, they believed that the "inner light"—the voice of God speaking directly to the heart—was more important than knowing God through listening to scholarly sermons and studying the Bible.

The Quakers, then, had a religious system that almost everybody else found objectionable. The Boston Puritans ran them out, and when some of them refused to leave, executed them. The English did not want them at home, and even Roger Williams, who had established in Rhode Island a colony dedicated to religious freedom, disliked them, although he tolerated their presence. Penn himself was once jailed for his beliefs.

Naturally, the Quakers had for some time been looking to the New World as a place where they might found a colony of their own. In 1674, there came available a large piece of land in what is now the state of New Jersey. The development of this colony is so complicated that even historians have trouble making sense of what happened there. Originally it had been given to the duke of York as part of the New York holdings he had been given by his brother, Charles II. The land passed through several hands, and was eventually divided roughly in half into West and East Jersey. In 1674, two Quakers bought a large piece of land in East Jersey. There were quarrels. William Penn was asked to settle the argument, and in the course of doing so, it occurred to him that the area might be a good place for a Quaker haven in America. But the situation in the Jerseys was a "muddle of perplexity," and eventually Penn gave up on it.

He turned his attention instead to the land west of New Jersey that we now know as Pennsylvania. Even though he was one of those despised Quakers, Penn had managed to maintain his friendship with the royal brothers, Charles an Anglican, and James a Catholic. In 1681, through clever diplomacy, he managed to get a charter for a new colony from Charles II. With this charter he became absolute proprietor of a vast chunk of the American wilderness. His powers were huge. He could promulgate laws with the assent of the freemen of the colony, and he could set up courts and hand down decisions.

Penn intended to call the new colony New Wales, but the government turned down this idea. Penn then decided on Sylvania, a Latin term meaning a wooded area. The government stuck Penn's name on the word, and thus we have Pennsylvania.

The English by now had had a good deal of experience at putting together colonies. Penn had pamphlets printed and translated into French, Dutch, and German, meant to attract colonists. He persuaded Charles also to give him the area now known as Delaware, so he would have direct access to the sea. He picked out a site for a capital city that would be high, and had water deep enough for a port. He had the city laid out in a grid pattern, and in line with Quaker simplicity named the streets First Street, Second Street, and so forth. He called the city Philadelphia—the City of Brotherly Love.

Penn was a Quaker who had been jailed for his religion and had a very strong belief in individual liberties—the rights he felt all Englishmen should have. There would be freedom of religion, trial by jury, regular elections. Moreover, Penn wanted his colony to deal fairly with the Indians, and buy land from them, rather than simply run them off it.

Pennsylvania was not to be a democracy in our modern sense. Penn could veto legislation, and over him was the king, who also had a say about certain things. But Penn's scheme was honorable and well thought out. Nonetheless, he almost immediately ran into problems. For one thing, there were already English settlers in portions of Penn's colony, particularly the three counties that would become Delaware. These people resented being taken over. Additionally, recruits from Wales, Ger-

A painting by Edward Hicks in the primitive style very common to the day in America, showing William Penn's treaty with the Indians in Pennsylvania.

many, Ireland, and Scotland did not come over singly, but in groups. They did not want to mingle with the Quakers, but wished rather to set up more or less independent towns and counties of their own on their own land. Inevitably, they began to quarrel, not only with Penn's government, but among themselves.

Penn himself had expected to move to Pennsylvania and live out his life there, and he did come over in 1682. But after a couple of years he was forced to return to England to deal with matters affecting Pennsylvania, and he did not get back to America until 1699. He found

A facsimile of a treaty with Indian tribes, in this case the Treaty of Fort Stanwix. Each Indian used his personal animal sign for his signature.

that the colony had grown astonishingly. In fifteen years Philadelphia had doubled in size to five thousand inhabitants. Its buildings were brick and stone, and they were filled with fine furniture, carpets, silver. The city was rapidly catching up to Boston and New York as a center not only for commerce, but for very un-Quakerly elegance as well.

The countryside was blooming, too. The rich soil, worked by industrious Quakers, was producing plentiful surplus crops for export to the Caribbean and Europe. It should be borne in mind that most immigrants came as indentured servants, who had to work in a kind of semislavery for a number of years, usually seven, before they were free to find a piece of land and set up farms of their own. The work, for nearly everybody, was hard; life, particularly on the western frontier, was not easy. But compared with places elsewhere, Pennsylvania was a prosperous land. And, uniquely among the seventeenth-century colonies, though perhaps not surprisingly in view of Quaker pacifism, for seventy-two years Penn's policies managed to avoid wars with Indians.

But beneath the prosperity was endless bickering. For one thing, during Penn's absence the colonists had tried to enlarge the power of the assembly and reduce the power of the commissioners Penn had left in charge. The three lower counties of Delaware were scheming to break away. Anglicans, whose church had aided in the persecution of the Quakers, were increasing in numbers and in wealth.

For another, many thousands of Scots, Germans, Welsh, and other ethnic groups clustered here and there about the colony insisted on speaking their own languages, following the customs they had brought from home, and generally putting their own interests first. Once again Penn might have solved things, but in 1701 he had to return to England. Before he went the colonists rammed down his throat a change in government, which made the elected assembly the primary power in the colony. At the same time the three lower counties demanded to be separated off as the colony of Delaware. Penn did not like either idea, but he gave in. He did not really have much choice, but he was probably willing to do so anyway, because there was a likelihood that the king was going to take over the colony and Penn wanted the colonists to have as much power as possible if that happened.

The freedom in Pennsylvania was a strong attraction for immigrants. Many people in Europe were still living essentially as serfs—dwelling in

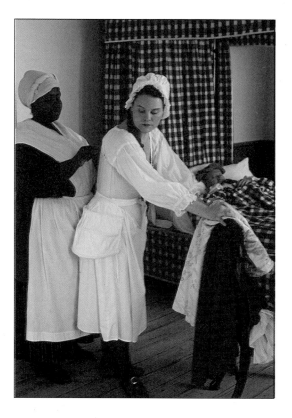

A reenactment from Williamsburg shows a servant, presumably a slave, helping a woman to dress. Fashion called for elaborate dress; the servant is buttoning the dress up the back.

hovels, eating the poorest kind of food, hedged in by the rules and regulations of the lords over them. Even the rough life of a Pennsylvania farmer seemed like heaven to them, and Germans in particular began to immigrate to the colony in large numbers. During the 1700s the population of Pennsylvania exploded. In the fifty years after 1700 the numbers jumped from 17,950 to 119,666. As ever, the immigrants settled into their own ethnic enclaves—the English in the east, the Germans in the north, the Scotch-Irish in the west, although there was much overlapping. There was as well a substantial population of Africans, nearly all of them slaves. Pennsylvania was certainly, by the early 1700s, the most diverse of the colonies, with lots of people speaking languages other than English. Ethnic groups were further broken down by religions. Among the Germans, for example, there were the Mennonites, the Dunkards, the Schwenkfelders, and the Moravians, some of whose descendants still adhere to the old ways. There were Anglicans in Philadelphia, as well as Presbyterian Scotch-Irish.

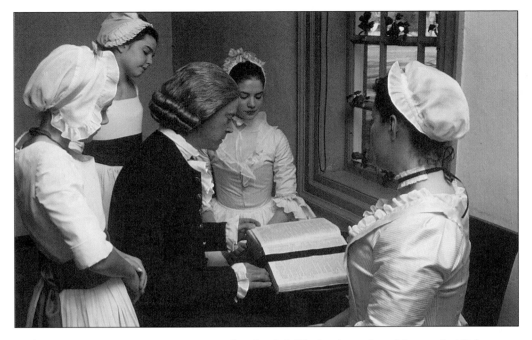

Religion was an important part of colonial life in America. Not only did people attend church frequently, but in many homes the father read something from the Bible to the family every day.

Penn's vision of peaceful relations with Indians was also badly blurred in his absence. The thousands of immigrants wanted land and there were huge profits to be made by the speculators who wanted to sell it to them. But the Delaware Indians stood astride the rich frontier. The government, still dominated by the Quakers, who had become the minority, was committed against war. They could, however, find surrogates in the mighty Iroquois of the Six Nations, and under this threat, the Delaware were persuaded to leave the areas coveted by land-hungry Europeans.

The problems confronting Pennsylvania were typical of what was going on in the colonies in general. The basic point is that three different groups had three different ideas of what the colonies were there for, and how they should be run. The king and his government saw the colonies

Many white Americans of the 1700s were prosperous. Few Americans ever went hungry, and the well-to-do, like the husband and wife in this reenactment, ate very well. Because vegetables were in short supply except during the season, Americans ate a great deal of meat. It was common for people to eat more than one kind of meat at a meal.

as branches of England. According to them, the people there were English subjects, and could be taxed to provide income for the English government.

The *investors,* on the other hand, had put a lot of money into developing the colonies, and they believed that first and foremost they ought to get their money back through rents or profits on products coming out of the colonies, like tobacco, rice, timber, furs.

Finally, the *colonists* living in America had come over to better themselves. They were doing the hard work of clearing the land and farming it, and they resented having to pay rents or taxes, which they frequently could not afford in any case. More and more, as time passed, the colonists saw the countryside around them in America as "theirs." No matter that the proprietors like William Penn, Lord Shaftesbury, or Lord Baltimore officially owned their colony, and that the king ruled in a general way over all: the settlers were actually living on the land, plowing the earth, harvesting the corn, digging wells, building houses and barns, and raising their children in the Carolinas, Massachusetts, Pennsylvania. They could not help but feel it belonged to them.

Houses were cold in the winter, even in Virginia. The curtains around beds like this one could be drawn to keep out the drafts. In this reenactment a sick man is being tended by his wife.

The conflicts between these three groups of people—the colonists, the proprietors, and the English government—were thus built into the situation. They would eventually lead to serious trouble.

From William Penn's point of view, the colony had not been a success. He had hoped to establish a colony of gentle, loving Quakers that would, not incidentally, produce a profit for him. He had, in fact, exhausted his wealth on Pennsylvania, and had not created the harmonious province he

Cooking was done over an open fire for the most part. Here a bird is being roasted on a spit while other foods are being cooked in pots hanging above the coals.

In fashionable families, it was expected that people would be musical. There was little professional entertainment; people had to amuse themselves. Here a slave tends the fire while the performers take a break from playing.

had hoped for. But from the viewpoint of history, Penn's colony had been successful, for it was filling up with people, and growing wealthy in farm products, especially wheat, and a healthy commerce centered on the great city on the Delaware River.

CHAPTER V

The French and the English in North America

The two developments in America which we have been looking at—the maturing of the colonies and the struggle among European nations for control of the territory—were beginning to run together, like two streams merging to create a mighty river. To see how that happened, let us stand back and take a look at the situation in North America as it looked from the palaces of kings in London, Madrid, Paris, and elsewhere.

By the early 1700s it had become clear to the Europeans that there was a lot of money to be made out of the colonies. This had not always been so: as we have seen, early investors like William Penn and Lord Baltimore lost heavily in their colonial gambles. But the colonies were shipping millions of pounds worth of goods out each year; somehow, there ought to be profit in it for the kings and princes of Europe who—in their view—owned it.

And the European princelings needed money. As ever, they were constantly jockeying for power in order to glorify themselves; wars were frequent, and wars were expensive. More often than not, European kings and queens were heavily in debt, always scrambling to find new sources of money.

So far as eastern North America was concerned, the little Swedish effort in Delaware had been ended by Peter Stuyvesant. The English in turn had taken over Stuyvesant's Dutch base in what became New York. The Spanish were boxed out by the English colonists in Georgia and the Carolinas, and the French settlements in New Orleans and up the Mississippi. By the early 1700s, there were only two European players in the game for North America east of the Mississippi River: England and France.

This way of thinking of course ignored several million other people who had some concern in North America: the colonists, and the Indians they were displacing. But that, as we have seen in the case of

By the middle of the 1700s, the British colonies in North America had come a long way from their rough beginnings a century earlier. Handsome public buildings, such as this hospital in Virginia, were going up everywhere.

THE FRENCH AND THE ENGLISH IN NORTH AMERICA   55

By these years, American ladies and gentlemen of the upper classes felt themselves to be equal to their English counterparts. They wore elegant clothing, which often was imported from England, lived in grand houses, and had their portraits painted. Here are two such people, Samuel Caw and Mary Blair Braxton. They were both from the Virginia aristocracy, which had a high opinion of itself.

Pennsylvania, was the way the European powers thought: the colonists were there for the convenience of the monarchs of Europe and their wealthy allies; and the Indians were not there at all.

The primary interest of France in North America was still the fur trade. There were French farming settlements along the St. Lawrence, of course, and three well-established towns, Quebec, Montreal, and Trois-Rivières. A small iron industry had been founded, and fishing off the coast was always profitable. But fur was the real moneymaker. Concentrating on fur, the French did not encourage settlement, but spread out along the rivers to trade with the Indians. One important fact was that in England, during the 1600s especially, there was a good deal of unemployment; it seemed sensible to the rulers to drain off what they saw as an excess of population by sending the poor and unemployed to America. The French, on the other hand, believed that they could not afford to drain themselves of people, and as a consequence did not encourage French subjects to settle in America. In the coming struggle between the English and French for control of North America, the English had a great advantage in numbers, which also meant an advantage in wealth.

But the French had the strategic advantage. They had established strong points on the coast in the Newfoundland area, along the St. Lawrence, and then down the Mississippi. In 1718, they put a plug in the mouth of the Mississippi with the founding of New Orleans. New Orleans and the Louisiana countryside around it was, during the whole of French rule, in chaos, with an unruly population filled with soldiers and criminals sent out from France, newly imported African slaves, and a large population of racially mixed people with white, Indian, and black ancestry, some free and some slave. Nonetheless, from its New Orleans base and strong points at Natchez and elsewhere along the Mississippi, France controlled shipping on the river. Effectively, only the French could bring goods, like timber and fur, out of the vast center of North America. With its control of the St. Lawrence and the Mississippi, the French had the English encircled.

Of particular interest to the French by the early 1700s was the area known as Ohio—roughly what is today all the land south of the Great Lakes, east of the Mississippi River stretching down to the Gulf of Mexico. The territory was cut with rivers, including the mighty Ohio, which allowed for good transportation through it; it was well populated

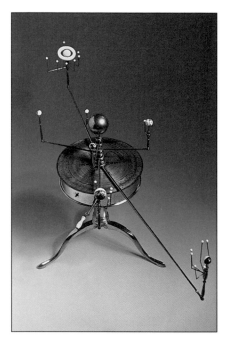

The prosperity of both England and its colonies depended heavily on trade. Americans imported huge quantities of English manufactured goods: both useful items like this navigational instrument and the gentlemen's tool chests, and purely frivolous items, such as this fancy ladies' fan.

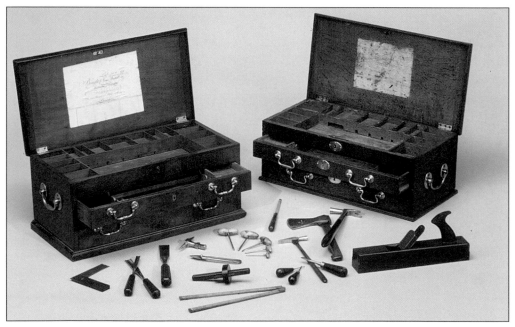

by a number of rivalrous Indian tribes, who wanted to trade furs for European goods, especially guns; the soil was very fertile, which mattered little to the French but would matter a good deal later on; and it was difficult for the English to get across the formidable Allegheny Mountains.

In England, the first steps toward bringing some order to the American colonies came late in the 1600s, when James II became king on the death of his brother Charles. We remember that James, when he was duke of York, had sent Richard Nicolls with his little fleet to drive the Dutch off the huge piece of land Charles had given James. James II was better informed about the colonies than many European rulers, and had a long-standing interest in them. Under him the English government began to realize that it had, almost by accident, come into possession of some immensely valuable property in the New World. They would act to gain control of it.

Among other things, the British government now began to take the colonies away from the proprietors and investors who had founded many of them, and put them under the direct control of the king and Parliament. As early as 1624, King James I had been forced to step in and take over Virginia to end a chaotic situation there. New York had been given to James as duke of York, and when he became king it automatically became a Crown colony. In 1684, James revoked the Massachusetts charter, and turned it, too, into a Crown colony. He then cobbled together something that was called the Dominion of New England, throwing together the New England colonies along with New York and New Jersey under one governor. The colonists bitterly protested this scheme, which threatened their independence, and when James was deposed in 1688 in favor of William and Mary, the Dominion of New England was dropped. But the net effect was to make Massachusetts a Crown colony, too. And so it went: one after another the old charters were revoked, and most of the colonies were put under the direct rule of the king. However, Pennsylvania and Maryland remained proprietary colonies until the

In exchange for the British goods Americans needed or simply wanted, they sent in trade huge quantities of raw materials and foodstuffs. Particularly important were crops of various kinds—rice, tobacco, cotton from the south, wheat and other grains from the north.

American Revolution, and Connecticut and Rhode Island began and continued as virtually autonomous charter colonies.

But James II's reign was brief. He was a Roman Catholic, and by favoring his fellow religionists, he upset most English people, who had long seen Roman Catholicism as the religion of their enemies, the French and Spanish. James II was forced from the throne, and was replaced by a Protestant Dutchman, William of Orange, whose wife, Mary, was James's daughter, but also a Protestant.

William took the English throne in part to bring England in on the side of Holland in yet another of the wars brewing on the European continent, and his interest in the colonies was secondary. Nonetheless, Holland had for a century and a half built its wealth and power on its colonies in the Far East, and William was accustomed to dealing with colonial problems. Under William and Mary, the Crown and Parliament determined to further systematize its colonial empire. William commissioned a Board of Trade with authority to supervise fisheries in American waters and colonial trade. It could also review all legislation by colonial assemblies and recommend disallowance, and nominate colonial officials, including governors. During William's reign the board exercised great influence.

Something similar was going on with the French holdings in North America. The French government was much more autocratic than was the English one. The French king could rule much as he wanted to, without limits set by a legislature. Louis XIV, who was king of France for much of the period we are discussing, was important in raising France as a major power in Europe. He was advised by a brilliant official, Jean-Baptiste Colbert. They turned New France, as the French domain in North America was called, into a royal province, governed by officials appointed by the king.

The rise of France as a power in Europe under the imperious Louis XIV was very threatening to the English. It appeared to them that the very aggressive French would take over where they could, interfering with England's own aspirations to glory. By 1660, the two nations were on a collision course in Europe; by chance, they had become the only two European combatants left in the battle for North America east of the Mississippi. What happened next must be seen as only one part of a rivalry between France and England that would lead to sporadic fighting for over a century.

In North America the battling was at first over control of the lucrative fur trade. Furs had to be brought out from the American interior by boats along waterways that reached deep into Indian territory. France, through its vast network of Indian allies, controlled the Mississippi, the St. Lawrence Seaway, and the Great Lakes region, and had a great advantage there. It was clear to the English that if they were to gain control of the interior, they would have to drive the French out of their forts along these water routes. In this they might have the help of the colonists, who also wanted to share in the fur trade.

We must remember that the main concern of the warring nations was always the power struggle in Europe; the colonies in the New World were often used merely as trading cards at the peace treaties that settled these wars. We can look at one of these wars as an example of how it worked. In 1739, England got into a scrap with Spain when a British seaman lost an ear in a minor naval skirmish. This episode escalated into the War of Jenkins' Ear, and when it merged with the British conflict with France was called the War of the Austrian Succession. The American phase of it was known as King George's War, after the English king of the time. As ever, the main concern of the European powers was Europe, but the war slopped over into northern New England. For the Americans, the most important event of King George's War was a combined effort of British and Americans against the French stronghold on Cape Breton Island. The island stood at the mouth of the Gulf of St. Lawrence and was thus the gate to the water route into the heart of New France. It was guarded by Fort Louisbourg; and if it could be taken by the English, the French would be hindered in their trade.

Governor William Shirley of Massachusetts, who of course represented the British government, persuaded the Massachusetts assembly to vote him money and men for an attack on Fort Louisbourg. He argued that the French possession of the stronghold allowed it to control half of the lucrative fishing industry in the North Atlantic. Besides, Shirley suggested, undoubtedly the Crown would pay the expenses when the war was

It was not only the wealthy who were prospering. Ordinary people, mostly independent family farmers, were also improving themselves. Settlers were pushing out into the wilderness and carving out farms there. This print was made in 1786, but the farm had been established some time before. The desire for land across the Appalachian Mountains brought the French and English into conflict and triggered the French and Indian War.

over. New York, Pennsylvania, and New Jersey helped with equipment and food, and in March 1745, some ninety ships with three thousand volunteers under a popular but inexperienced man named William Pepperell, left for Cape Breton Island.

It was a considerable gamble: Fort Louisbourg was considered the strongest fort in America. The British force approaching it was, as one historian has said, "an amateur general with an amateur army." Fortunately, a small force of ships from the Royal Navy joined the expedition. The ships blockaded Cape Breton Island, so that neither reinforcements nor supplies could come in. Pepperell's little army took the French by surprise and landed on the island without a fight.

The American troops now placed Fort Louisbourg under siege. For weeks they battered the fort with cannon fire, some from French guns outside the fort which they had taken. Finally, with most of the walls blown down and many of the French cannons destroyed, the Americans prepared to charge the fort. The French, seeing that their position was hopeless, surrendered.

It was, one historian said, "a remarkable feat of arms for inexperienced militiamen." When the news of the victory reached the colonies there were celebrations everywhere. Although the blockade by the British navy had been crucial, it was nonetheless an American victory over what had been the strongest fort in North America. And then, in 1748, a peace was negotiated in Europe. In the bargaining, the English handed Cape Breton Island and Fort Louisbourg back to the French. The Americans were left bitterly resentful at having their great victory—which they won at the cost of hundreds of lives—torn from them, but there was nothing they could do about it.

Thus, after sixty years of battling, the struggle for North America remained unsettled. The British, at least in theory, had possession of a huge piece of land around Hudson Bay at the top of the continent, although in practice it remained largely unsettled by Europeans. The French held an equally huge crescent running from Cape Breton Island at the mouth of the St. Lawrence, inland to the Great Lakes, and down the Mississippi to the rough little town of New Orleans. Below the French possessions were the thirteen English colonies from Maine—which was part of Massachusetts—to Georgia.

The French had their advantage in their control of major waterways. Further, they had done a much better job than the English in forging alliances with the Indians. They could count on the numerous Ojibwe north of the Great Lakes, Choctaw close to the Gulf of Mexico, and thousands of warriors in between.

The English, however, had a great advantage in population. There were only about seventy thousand settlers in all of the vast area called New France. The English colonies had a population of 1.2 million people, and more were pouring in daily. Moreover, these colonies were not rough frontier settlements, but were well-established places. Some families in the English colonies had been in America for five or six generations. The seacoast ports were turning into cosmopolitan cities, and the countryside was rapidly being carpeted with farms. The English were not merely firmly dug in; they were expanding.

Inevitably, the mountain barrier running like a spine along the back ends of the English colonies was being pierced. Trappers and mountain men going across the Appalachians to trade for furs were cutting into the valuable French fur trade. Farmers in crowded seacoast areas, where the soil was already growing thin or had been taken up and monopolized by a few large plantation owners and land speculators, were eyeing the rich bottomland of the Ohio Territory. The English government in London realized that as a practical matter, if they settled the Ohio Territory it would become English property. It gave huge grants of land to speculators willing to settle them, and the speculators were in turn sending people into the Ohio Territory to look for good sites for development.

The French, of course, were not about to sit still and let the English simply take over this immensely valuable land. In 1752, they sent to Canada a tough and able new governor, Marquis Duquesne. He sent a

From the first illustrated book about Canada, by André Thevet. The French were not as interested in settling North America as the English were, but saw it mainly as a source of products such as timber and furs. Here hunters on snowshoes are chasing animals in the northern forest.

small force, mostly of his Indian allies, into the Ohio River Valley. They burned out a village of Indians who had been trading furs with the English, and boiled and ate their leader. Duquesne then began to build a chain of small forts through the area at river junctions where they could control the movement of traders and furs.

Now it was the turn of the English to grow worried. A new governor named Robert Dinwiddie had just come to Virginia. He decided to send a small party out into the wilderness to ward off the French. The man he chose to lead the party was a tall, rangy, athletic twenty-one-year-old, who had worked as a surveyor in the Shenandoah Valley, and knew something about traveling in rough country. His name was George Washington. He would light the spark that fired the French and Indian War.

CHAPTER VI

The French and Indian War

Most Americans are well aware of the role George Washington played in winning the Revolution, and in starting the new country off as first president. His role in the French and Indian War, which led directly to the Revolution, is not so well known, but it was very important.

In October 1753, Washington set off into the wilderness with his small party to tell the French that the English did not view kindly the forts they were building in the Ohio Valley. He gave the commanders the message that George II, the English king, claimed the Ohio region, and wanted the French to leave. The French commanders were as polite, but of course they had no intention of leaving. Before he came back, Washington explored the so-called forks of the Ohio. This is the place where the Monongahela and Allegheny Rivers join to form the Ohio—where Pittsburgh now stands. It was obviously a key point in the Ohio Valley river system over which both men and goods must travel. The French, Washington learned, planned to build a fort there.

In December Washington started back to Virginia to make his report. The weather was bitterly cold. In order to move quickly he set off with one frontiersman and an Indian guide, who claimed to know of a shortcut. They had not gone very far when they reached a snow-filled clearing. The Indian darted forward, swiveled around, raised his rifle, and fired at Washington. Says one of Washington's biographers, James Flexner, "The bullet moved through the utter emptiness without changing the history of the world." The Indian had missed.

Washington and his companion raced forward and pinned the Indian into the snow before he could reload. The other man wanted to kill the Indian before he could call in his friends to help. But Washington did not like unnecessary killing, and would not allow it.

After a terrible trek through freezing weather, they reached the last stream they would have to cross before coming out of the wilderness. It was filled with great chunks of ice borne along by the current. They built a raft and set off into the icy stream. Almost immediately they were thrown into the water. They scrambled onto an island, and there they spent the night, sleeping in clothes frozen solid. Fortunately, in the morning they found the stream frozen across, and they could walk to safety.

Washington reported to Dinwiddie that the French planned to build a fort at the forks of the Ohio. Dinwiddie realized that the Virginians must build a fort there before the French did. He sent out a workforce to do the job. The French arrived with troops, told the Virginia workers to go home, and started building Fort Duquesne at the forks.

Meanwhile, Dinwiddie had sent George Washington out with a detachment of troops to protect the workers. He was camped one night when he learned that there was a small force of Frenchmen ahead. He marched on them, and attacked. Ten of the French were killed and others captured.

The attack was a very foolish move on Washington's part. The French, so they claimed, had been coming as diplomats to negotiate with the Virginians and had not intended to fight. In revenge, they sent a much larger force against the Virginians. Washington was young, inexperienced, and foolhardy. Instead of sensibly retreating, he scratched together a little stockade he called Fort Necessity and there made a stand. It was not until a third of his men were dead or wounded that he surrendered. The French kindly sent him and his men home.

This little episode, the first of many in which George Washington would play a major and significant role, was really a very minor affair compared with many other battles in America. But it was a crucial one, for it triggered the showdown between the English and French for control of North America. Before it was over, the European powers would be, for once, truly concerned over events in the New World. To be sure, their interest was in building their own empires. But in so doing they were also acting in behalf of their own colonists—the relative handful of French trappers, traders, and farmers along the long French waterways, and much larger number of English settlers in the seacoast colonies.

Oddly enough, George Washington came out of the battle of Fort Necessity a hero to his fellow Virginians: he had defeated one group of Frenchmen and had held out against a much larger force for hours. Washington himself said, "I have heard the bullets whistle, and believe me, there is something charming in the sound." George Washington was beginning to learn his trade as a soldier. Nonetheless, the battle at Fort Necessity had been a defeat.

The British government in London was not yet ready for another war with the French. But they were not willing to concede the Ohio country and its fur trade, either. They sent to America General Edward Braddock with two small regiments. In Virginia Braddock added Washington as an aide. However rash the young man, he knew the territory.

In June 1755, Braddock set off for Fort Duquesne, cutting a road through the forest for his cannons and supply wagons. Braddock should not have had any trouble taking the fort, for he had a much larger force. But ten miles from Fort Duquesne, a much smaller French force encoun-

George Washington, painted in the uniform of the Virginia militia by the famous artist Charles Willson Peale. Washington probably wore a uniform of this kind when he fought Braddock outside Fort Dusquesne.

tered Braddock's advance guard. The English officers in charge made some mistakes; the troops panicked. The French and their Indian allies spread out in the woods into a crescent formation and pounded the English troops from their hiding places with musket fire. Washington had two horses shot from under him; four bullets passed through his clothes without hitting him. Miraculously, he was not hurt in the withering fire. But Braddock was wounded, and died, leaving Washington as the surviving officer in charge. He managed to lead the remnants of the little British army out of the woods and back to Virginia.

Once again, Washington was acclaimed as a hero, despite a defeat. The story was widely reported around the colonies, and Washington began to get a national reputation as a brave and resourceful soldier.

Perhaps even more important, at about the same time William Johnson, a New Yorker and an experienced Indian agent, commanded what Americans chose to see as a victory in northern New York. In fact, Johnson failed to take his objective, a fort at Crown Point on Lake Champlain, but when the French chased him south to Lake George, he managed to beat back their attacks.

Nonetheless, it appeared that the French could beat the British. Over the next years the war wandered on, with almost all the victories going to the French. The Indians, seeing nothing but English defeats, began to move to the French side. The Delaware, many of whom had moved to the Ohio Valley under pressure from Pennsylvanians and Iroquois, saw the French as allies against further English expansion. Until now at peace with Pennsylvania, they began to attack frontier outposts there. Even the Iroquois, longtime allies of the English, began to flirt with the French.

Then, in 1756, William Pitt became chief minister of England. Pitt is today seen as one of England's greatest statesmen: Pittsburgh was named for him. Up until this point the French and English, as usual, had concentrated their attention on warfare in Europe. Among other things, the French had taken the German principality of Hanover, which, as it happened, was ruled by the British King George II. The French, aided by the Spanish, after 1762, were also pressing the most important of the German states, Prussia, under Frederick II. With a few more victories they would

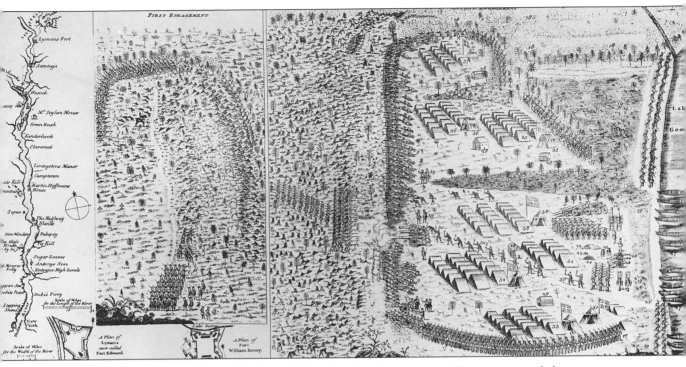

A schematic drawing of the Battle of Lake George. At left is a map of the Hudson River as it approaches Lake George, the lower part of the famous water route to the St. Lawrence River. Lake George was only a short portage from the southern end of Lake Champlain, the next portion of the water route. Possession of this portage area was critical to control of this route. The area was fought over in both the French and Indian and Revolutionary Wars.

be able to dominate Europe. So far as George II and most British politicians were concerned, the great thing was to stop the French on the continent of Europe; what happened in America was far less important to them.

William Pitt had a different idea. He saw that England by itself could never become a dominant power in Europe; it was simply too small. On the other hand, if England were able to build a great overseas empire, producing wealth in cattle, grains, sugar, timber, cotton, metal ores, and everything else that people everywhere needed, it could become a great and powerful nation.

Hanging on to America was crucial to Pitt's plan. He now decided to throw a great deal of Britain's armed forces into America. It was the first—but not the last—time that a European power had put the North American colonies first in their thinking. Pitt sent across to America a large number of fresh troops, and a big portion of the Royal Navy. He also promoted some young officers to take command pushing aside older ones he felt were incompetent. Two of these new generals were John Forbes and Jeffrey Amherst, who were jumped into command over the heads of many others.

Pitt saw that the capture of Quebec was crucial to the defeat of the French. As somebody said at the time, "When the

William Pitt the Elder is still considered one of the most important of England's statesmen. His strategy was important in winning the French and Indian War.

Lord Jeffrey Amherst was a young general promoted by Pitt over older officers. He beat the French at Louisbourg and again on the Champlain water route north.

spring is diverted or cut off, the river must dry up. Such is the position of Quebec that it is absolutely the key to French America...."

But taking Quebec would be no easy matter. It was situated on a rocky cliff on the St. Lawrence River. The cliff was three hundred fifty feet high. The beach at the base was narrow. There was not much room there for troops to land, maneuver, and then climb up the rocky cliff face. But the English knew that if they took Quebec, they would unlock the door to New France.

Before Quebec could be attacked, the British would have to clear away the approaches. One of these was the celebrated Fort Louisbourg on Cape Breton Island. General Amherst was sent to attack Louisbourg with a formidable force, including a substantial fleet. By good luck he managed to land some troops on the island. He set up a siege and for almost two months British cannons blasted at the fort, until its walls were rubble. Finally the French general surrendered. However, he had managed to hold up the British advance for two precious months.

At the same time the British attacked Fort Ticonderoga, at the critical portage between Lake George and Lake Champlain, on the water route north into New France. The attack failed. With winter coming, Amherst and other British leaders realized they would have to put off the attack on Quebec until the next year, 1758. The English spent the rest of the summer attacking small defensive points where they could. The most important of these was an attack by General Forbes on Fort Duquesne at the forks of the Ohio. One English effort to capture the fort had ended in a disastrous defeat by Indians who then left the area. Two months later Forbes would try again.

We must remember that although these British forces were built around British army regulars, they also included many regiments of Americans and hundreds of Indians. Forbes had under his command sixteen hundred British regulars, twenty-seven hundred men from Pennsylvania, and a force of twenty-six hundred men under Colonel George Washington. Forbes was desperately ill and had to travel through the wilderness in a sling hung between two horses. But he pressed forward and closed in on Fort Duquesne. When the French realized the might of the force they were facing, they sank their cannons in the river, burned the fort, and escaped. Forbes came upon a blackened ruin. Fort Duquesne, the latch to the fertile Ohio country, had been unlocked, this time without a fight. Poor Forbes died before he could return to England to receive acclaim for his victory.

The conquest of Fort Duquesne changed the attitude of the Indians. The early victories of the French had made the Indians wary of siding with the British. But with the British victories at Duquesne, Louisbourg, and other places, they began turning away from the French. It is likely, too,

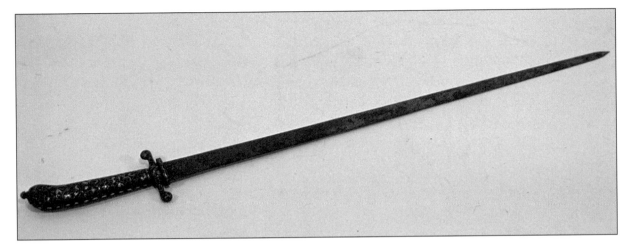

A French short saber of the type in use at the time of the French and Indian War.

that the French had run short of powder and shot to supply the Indians.

With spring the British and American armies began the attack on Quebec. General Amherst, with a large force of British augmented by American troops, began moving up the by now much fought-over water passage north—that is, up the Hudson, a short distance across land to Lake George; up this lake, and then another short portage over land to Lake Champlain. Champlain runs up to what is now the Canadian border, from where the Richelieu River courses to the St. Lawrence. Meanwhile, another British force would travel up the St. Lawrence directly to Quebec. This army would be under the command of General James Wolfe, another of the bright, aggressive young officers William Pitt had sent to America.

Amherst, pushing up the Champlain water route, found French resistance slight. The French commander had been told to save his forces for the defense of Quebec and Montreal. Amherst remained in the area perfecting his defenses and failed to march out to join Wolfe.

On June 26, 1759, the other British army, under Wolfe, reached the

Quebec area. Wolfe landed his forces at several points to the east of Quebec. His troops dug in and began to bombard the city on top of the rocky cliff. Over the next few weeks Wolfe tried again and again to make a landing on the beaches below and to the east of Quebec, from which he could make a direct assault on the city. Each attempt failed. The French inside had plenty of supplies and a sizable number of troops who were commanded by one of France's best generals, Louis Joseph, marquis de Montcalm.

For weeks Wolfe studied the beaches around Quebec. It seemed that only the beaches to the east of the city offered any chance of making a landing. The land to the west of the city was all steep cliffs with very narrow beaches. Moreover, British troops would have to sail past the city, under its guns to reach the western beaches.

Finally some of Wolfe's junior officers convinced him that he had to attack on the western side of the city, despite the rocky cliffs there. On top of the cliffs to the west of the city was a broad, flat area known as the Plains of Abraham. If troops could get up there, they would have Quebec cut off from its supply bases up the St. Lawrence to the west. Montcalm would be forced to come out of the fort and fight, and the British thought they could win in an open battle.

Wolfe was persuaded. Standing on the south side of the St. Lawrence peering through his spyglass, he carefully examined the narrow beach and steep cliffs leading up to the Plains of Abraham. Suddenly he noticed a narrow path winding up the cliff. There was the door to Quebec, he thought. It would have to be now or never, for the Canadian winter was closing in.

At about four o'clock in the morning on September 13, 1759, eighteen hundred troops were rowed ashore and landed on the narrow beach. Quickly they began climbing up the rocky cliff, as many as could clambering up the narrow path, others scrambling up the cliff by clinging to brush and rocks. The French had considered the approach impassable and it was lightly guarded. By dawn a formidable force of British soldiers was assembled on the Plains of Abraham outside the city of Quebec.

Hastily, the surprised Montcalm organized his troops to face the British. Indian and Canadian irregulars sniped at the British troops with muskets, but the troops stood fast. Each side had about forty-five hundred men, but the British troops were all experienced regulars, while the French army included a lot of hastily recruited Canadian farmers. Nonetheless, Montcalm was determined to fight—but perhaps he should not have. His supplies were getting low, and the British troops on the Plains of Abraham had cut him off from his bases.

At ten in the morning, sitting high on his horse above his troops, Montcalm gave the command to advance. His troops trotted forward. The British soldiers stood still, waiting. Wolfe darted everywhere, encouraging his troops. On came the French. Finally, when they were only about half the length of a football field from the British, they stopped and fired. Many British soldiers fell dead and wounded, but still they waited, unmoving.

The French came on again. Finally, when the French were hardly more than ten yards from them, the British troops fired. The French line fell into pieces, the dying men shrieking and groaning. The French troops broke and ran back toward the fort. The British troops charged with swords and bayonets, and soon the remains of the defeated force were pinned against the walls of the city in complete disorganization. Wolfe had won.

But in that brief battle James Wolfe had been shot in the chest. He died within a few minutes, but not before he knew he had won. What he would never know is that the brief battle on the Plains of Abraham would turn out to be one of the most important ever fought in North America, for it changed the course of American history.

Montcalm, too, was shot. He managed to stay on his horse and get into the city, but he died there the next day.

This famous painting shows the dying General Wolfe being carried off the battlefield. It was not painted from life, but was the artist's idea of what happened.

The French knew that they would soon be starved out, so theys quickly surrendered Quebec, and escaped with their forces in order to save them for the defense of Montreal farther down the river. But as the news spread through colonial America, and then to England, there were victory celebrations, bonfires, banquets. For over one hundred fifty years Quebec had been at the center of France's North America empire, and now it belonged to the British.

Montreal did not surrender until the next year, but when confronted by a vastly larger British force, gave up without a fight. Other French outposts quickly surrendered as well, and by 1763 the English were in possession of the vast land from the Arctic down to Florida, from the Atlantic to the Mississippi.

The French and Indian War, as we now call it, is not nearly so well known as some other wars the American people have been involved in. There are whole libraries full of books on the Civil War and World War II. Even very young schoolchildren know about the great events of the Revolution, such as Paul Revere's ride, the Battles of Lexington and Concord, the crossing of the Delaware by George Washington's troops to take Trenton, New Jersey. Of the French and Indian War most Americans know little.

Yet it was an event of immense importance. For one thing, the early battles at Fort Necessity and elsewhere made George Washington a national celebrity; it is generally agreed by historians that without Washington, the American Revolution might very well not have succeeded. It was the French and Indian War that brought Washington to the attention of Americans, and gave him the experience he needed to fight the British in the Revolution. For the second, the war showed that European forces were not as formidable as Americans had thought. They had seen William Johnson's Americans hold off the French at Lake George, while the vaunted British troops under Braddock had crumbled at Fort Duquesne. Perhaps the Americans were deluding themselves to some extent. Nonetheless, their experience in the French and Indian War made them believe that they might be able to take on the British and gave them the courage, sixteen years after the fall of Quebec, to try.

More significantly, if the British had not driven the French out of Canada, it would have been dangerous for Americans to try to break away from the British Empire on their own. Without the support of the mighty British army and navy the French, from their bastions in the north, would have been able to harass the English colonies to the south, and threaten their fishing fleets in the North Atlantic. They would have continued to scoop up much of the fur and fishing trade. They would have made alliances with the Indians, stirring them up against the English colonists. In sum, had the French remained a power in North America, they could have made life not just difficult, but dangerous to English colonials. On the other hand, had the French remained in control they might have become America's allies in a war against England as indeed they did in 1778.

Most significantly, so long as the French were in the Ohio Valley and occupied their chain of forts along the Mississippi, the English colonists could not have expanded their domain across the Appalachians into the fertile lands there. With Ohio blocked, there would have been no way for the English colonials to press to the Mississippi, then across to the plains beyond and the Pacific Coast. Had this movement to the west been halted, the United States would still consist of perhaps fifteen states bordering the Atlantic surrounded by French-speaking Americans.

The results of the war were not finally settled until the Treaty of Paris in 1763, between England, France, and Spain. In the negotiations various portions of North America and some Caribbean islands were swapped around. The British got all of North America to the Mississippi, including Spanish Florida, except two small islands off Newfoundland, which the French were allowed to keep as bases for their fishing fleet. Spain had allied herself with France, for reasons having to do with the war in Europe. In the swapping around at the Treaty of Paris, Spain lost Florida to England, and France gave New Orleans to Spain, along with territory France claimed west of the Mississippi, the vast region then called Louisiana. Various Caribbean islands were split between England and France. But what really mattered, in the end, was that the English colonies on the Atlantic were now free of the French menace, and no longer so desperately needed protection from the mighty British army and navy. And so it began to occur to a few Americans that they didn't need the English king and Parliament, either. Without that British victory on the Plains of Abraham none of this would have happened.

BIBLIOGRAPHY

Many of the books that are no longer in print may still be found in school or public libraries.

For Students

Carter, Alden R. *The Colonial Wars: Clashes in the Wilderness.* Danbury, Conn.: Franklin Watts, 1992.

Meltzer, Milton, ed. *The American Revolutionaries: A History in Their Own Words, 1750–1800.* New York: Thomas Y. Crowell, 1987.

Scott, John Anthony. *Settlers on the Eastern Shore: The British Colonies in North America, 1607–1750.* Library of American History Series. New York: Facts on File, 1991.

Smith, Carter, ed. *Battles in a New Land: A Sourcebook on Colonial America.* Brookfield, Conn.: Millbrook Press, 1991.

Washburne, Carolyn Kott. *A Multicultural Portrait of Colonial Life.* Tarrytown, N.Y.: Marshall Cavendish, 1993.

For Teachers

Dorn, Walter L. *Competition for Empire, 1740–1763*. New York: Harper and Row, 1940. (Out of print.)

Edmonds, Walter D. *The Musket and the Cross: The Struggle of France and England for North America*. Boston: Little, Brown, 1968.

Gipson, Lawrence H. *The British Empire Before the American Revolution*. 14 vols. New York: Alfred A. Knopf, 1936–1969. (Out of print.)

Leach, Douglas E. *Arms for Empire: A Military History of the British Colonies in North America, 1607–1763*. New York: Macmillan, 1973. (Out of print.)

Parkman, Francis. *Montcalm and Wolfe*. 2 vols. Boston: Little, Brown, 1884. Reprint. New York: Da Capo, 1995.

Peckham, Howard H. *Colonial Wars, 1689–1762*. Chicago: University of Chicago Press, 1965.

Wallace, Anthony F.C. *King of the Delawares: Teedyuscung, 1700–1763*. Philadelphia: University of Pennsylvania Press, 1949.

INDEX

British Board of Trade, 61
  Pennsylvania legislature, 44, 47
grants, land, 25–26, 65
Great Lakes, 57, 62, 64, 65
Gulf of Mexico, 57, 65
Gulf of the St. Lawrence, 62

Hanover, Germany, 72
Hartford, Connecticut, 22
Hicks, Edward, painting by, 45
Holland. *See* Dutch
home, colonial, **51**
Hudson, Henry, 21–22, 28, 30
Hudson Bay, 12, 64
Hudson River, 21, 22, 30, 33, 73, 77
Hudson River Valley, 12, 22, 28, 31
Huguenots, 35

immigrants, 44–45, 48–49
indentured servants, 47
Indians, 9–11, **11**, 12, **25, 26**, 55–56
  allies with the British, 76
  allies with the French, 62, 65, 71, 72, 76
  and Franciscan missionaries, 34
  fur trade with, 22, 28, 36, 39, 41, 57,
    59, 66
  Indian agent, 72
  in North America, 26–27, 55–56
  in Pennsylvania, 44, 49
  purchase of Manhattan Island from,
    22, 30
  and Stuyvesant, 28, **29**
  treaties of, **45, 46**
  trouble with colonists, 16, 17
  wars between tribes of, 26–27

indigo, 36
investors, British, 39, 50, 54, 59
Irish colonists, 45, 48
iron industry, 56
Iroquois Indians, 26–27, 49, 72
Italy, 24

James, Duke of York
  the Dutch and, 31, 32, 33
  as King James II, 59, 60
  Penn and, 42, 43, 44
James I, King of England, 59
James II, King of England, 59, 60.
    See also James, Duke of York
James River, 21
Jamestown, Virginia, **17**
Johnson, William, 72, 81

King George's War, 62

Lake Champlain, 72, 73, 75, 76, 77
Lake George, 77, 81
Lake George, Battle of, 72, **73**, 76
land grants, 25–26, 65
languages, 15, 33
Latin America, 41
Locke, John, 35
London, 25, 30, 54, 65, 70
Long Island, 16
  Dutch occupation of, 28, 30, 32
  English claims on, 22, 23
Louis XIV, King of France, 61
Louisiana, 57, 82

Madrid, 54

JAMES LINCOLN COLLIER is the author of a number of books both for adults and for young people, including the social history *The Rise of Selfishness in America*. He is also noted for his biographies and historical studies in the field of jazz. Together with his brother, Christopher Collier, he has written a series of award-winning historical novels for children widely used in schools, including the Newbery Honor classic, *My Brother Sam Is Dead*. A graduate of Hamilton College, he lives with his wife in New York City.

CHRISTOPHER COLLIER grew up in Fairfield County, Connecticut and attended public schools there. He graduated from Clark University in Worcester, Massachusetts and earned M.A. and Ph.D. degrees at Columbia University in New York City. After service in the Army and teaching in secondary schools for several years, Mr. Collier began teaching college in 1961. He is now Professor of History at the University of Connecticut and Connecticut State Historian. Mr. Collier has published many scholarly and popular books and articles about Connecticut and American history. With his brother, James, he is the author of nine historical novels for young adults, the best known of which is *My Brother Sam Is Dead*. He lives with his wife Bonnie, a librarian, in Orange, Connecticut.